THE IPHO

C000136891

GUIDE

YOUR COMPLETE IPHONE XR MANUAL FOR BEGINNERS, NEW IPHONE XR USERS AND SENIORS

Tech Analyst

Copyright @2019

TABLE OF CONTENT

8

How to Use this Book

Welcome! Thank you for purchasing this book and trusting us to lead you right in operating your new device. This book has covered every details and tips you need to know about the iPhone XR for to get the best from the device.

To better understand how the book is structured, I would advise you read from page to page after which you can then navigate to particular sections as well as make reference to a topic individually. This book has been written in the simplest form to ensure that every user understands and gets the best out of this book. The table of content is also well outlined to make it easy for you to reference topics as needed at the speed of light.

Thank you.

Introduction

The iPhone XR was launched in October 26, 2018 after the iPhone XS and XS Max and as at the time it was launched, the Apple company tagged it "the Cheapest iPhone device of the year." The price of the iPhone XR got several iPhone fans excited to own a new iPhone XR. However, being tagged cheap doesn't mean that the device lacks the high standard that the Apple brand is known with as the company equipped the smartphone with lots of abilities and features.

iPhone XR Specs

- OS: iOS 12
- Resolution: 1792 x 828
- Weight: 194g
- CPU: A12 Bionic
- Front camera: 7MP
- Rear camera: 12MP
- Resistance: IP67
- Screen size: 6.1-inch

- Dimensions: 150.9 x 75.7 x 8.3mm
- Storage: 64/128/256
- Colors: White, Blue, Black, Coral, Yellow, Red

Price of the iPhone XR

The iPhone was launched at the retail price of $749, which is what endeared several users to it against the iPhone XS and XS Max that were sold at $999 and $1,099 respectively. For an android user, this price may be high as there are quality android phones at lower prices like some brands of the Samsung. However, if you are an iPhone lover, this is definitely a good buy.

You would see the prices of the iPhone XR below depending on the storage capabilities that you desire

- $749 for 64 GB
- $799 for 128 GB

- $899 for 256 GB

iPhone XR iOS

The iPhone XR just like the XS and XS Max runs on the iOS 12 operating system. While you may think that the price of the iPhone means lesser quality from other iPhones released same year, be assured that Apple still gave the iPhone XR topnotch features and abilities.

iPhone XR Processor

The iPhone XR is on same A12 bionic chop with the X and XS. If we look at all the processors that Apple has used from inception till date, we can conclude that the A12 bionic processor is still their best decision yet. Apple says that the A12 bionic chip has been designed to power a minimum of 5 trillion operations per second.

Dust and Water Resistance

Like the iPhone XS and X, the XR does not go bad if it falls into water or gets covered by dust as the Apple company built the phones to withstand being in water up to one meter deep for as long as 30 minutes. However, as is normal with other devices, Apple has warned that this feature is not permanent as the phone's ability to resist dust and water can reduce with normal wear and tear.

What's New with the iPhone XR

For Apple to be able to give users that cheap price, they had to downgrade the iPhone XR a little compared to the XS. Although there are some features that are same with the XS like the iOS 12 operating system backed up by the strong A12 Bionic chipset inside. The notch on both devices have same front facing sensors and cameras, the dual speakers too is also in same location. The latest additions of the iPhone brand all have the home button missing including the iPhone XR.

For people who are not familiar with the iPhone series or if the iPhone XS and XR are not placed beside each other, it may be difficult to tell the difference, but there exists some difference between the two.

iPhone XR Camera

one impressive feature of the iPhone XR is the camera which is significantly higher than the iPhone X.

Although the iPhone XR camera has same standard lens with the XS, however, it does not have the telephoto second sensor, and one would need to do some tricks with software to make up for this.

One basic difference in the camera is that with the iPhone XR camera, you would be unable to zoom as far as you would like because of the portrait mode. You are still able to have portrait shots and keep the background attractively blurred to maintain focus on the subject, but you would not be able to take pictures of animals and objects in same way that an iPhone XS can.

This is because it is difficult for the software to easily identify the subjects using a single sensor while the extra hardware which makes the iPhone XS expensive, can be used to get more focus.

The Liquid Retina screen

Several users assumed that the iPhone XR would have the same OLED display like the other new releases, however, Apple thought different and launched the phone with an entirely new type of LCD, to give the phone an 'all screen' display.

Several users saw this feature as something from the past, but Apple referred to it as a view from the future. The iPhone XR is the first iPhone device to have the full face of the camera covered. This is the reason Apple called it the **"Liquid Retina Display."**

This "Liquid Retina Display" is also the first Apple's LCD device that comes with the Tap to Wake feature.

You may not see the screen to be as fanciful as the other devices that have the OLED display, however, the screen size of this phone is quite impressive and should make up for the LCD display.

Absence of 3D Touch on the XR

Every user of the new versions of the iPhone brand would be used to the 3D touch where you can open menus and activate several different features in the apps by simply pressing the screen hard. This 3D touch feature has been removed from the XR and replaced with the Haptic touch. Although this is slightly similar to the 3D touch, it just requires you to press a little harder to open apps or menus. To do this, simply press your desired application for some seconds until you feel some vibration. One of the limitations of this is that you cannot use this to view actions and widgets on your Home screen icons, but you can always access the widgets from the control center.

Chunkier design

The iPhone XR comes with a thicker design as well as chunkier bezels by the sides of the smartphone. You can only know the difference with the XS when you place both beside each other. When you look at the device, you may be unable to tell the size and weight as it looks like an updated version of the iPhone 8. Let's summarize to say that the iPhone XR is the all screen version of the iPhone 8 and even iPhone 7 with some added features.

Multiple colors

The iPhone is the first to come in several colors. The XR is available in six colors: white, red, blue, coral, yellow and black. This makes the iPhone XR an excellent choice if you are looking for an iPhone with fashion in mind.

Better Battery

The iPhone XR comes with an extra 90 minutes than the 8 Plus which is a big plus for iPhone lovers. The battery of the iPhone is able to last for a whole day before you would need to recharge. Battery life for most iPhone devices have been quite terribly and Apple have compensated users by ensuring that the iPhone XR comes with a better battery life. This iPhone XR is the first iPhone brand that you would not need to worry about battery drainage day to day and this alone gives it the feature of being tagged one of the greatest iPhone devices.

The iPhone XR has a battery size of 2,942 mAh while the iPhone XS runs on 2,658 mAh.
According to reports by Apple, below are the iPhone XR battery specifications:

- Up to 65 hours audio playback on wireless
- Up to 25 hours talk time on wireless
- Up to 16 hours video playback on wireless
- Up to 15 hours internet use

Apple also gave the bonus of wireless charging on the iPhone XR. This device gives you an extra

one and half hour battery life against the iPhone
8.

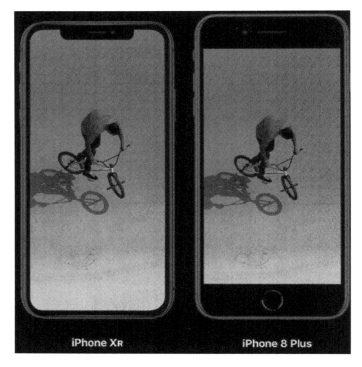

iPhone Xʀ   iPhone 8 Plus

Exclusive Wallpapers

Each iPhone XR device comes with pre-loaded
custom wallpapers designed to go with the
exterior of the smartphone. The wallpapers are
simply beautiful and are only exclusive to the
iPhone XR.

Other features of the iPhone XR include

- Introduction of Memoji
- 12-MP camera, the True Depth camera system with Face ID
- Wireless charging
- True Tone
- P3 wide color gamut
- Supports Dual SIM - one nano-SIM and one eSIM
- Bluetooth 5 as well as most recent updates in LTE.

CHAPTER 1

Getting Started: How to set up your iPhone XR

You can set up your new iPhone XR in various ways, whether you want to start anew, restore apps from another phone or import data and content from a phone that is not in the Apple family. First, let me explain what these three options mean for iPhone XR users.

Option 1: Starting anew means beginning the setting from scratch and this applies to people who have not used a smartphone before or a phone with internet services.

Option 2: You can import data from your old device that is not an Apple brand like Windows, Android or Blackberry using the Apple App in Google play, this is mostly for Android users. This option is suitable if you are moving to the iPhone brand newly from your android.

Steps to Setup the iPhone XR

- First step is to power on your new device by pressing and holding the side button. Once the screen comes up, on your screen, you would see the "Hello" greeting in various languages. This applies whether you have used an iPhone before or not.

- Next, a slider would show on the screen with a *Slide to Set Up* option, click on this option

- Choose your Language, Region and Country. It is important you select the right information as this would affect how information like date and time etc. is presented on the device.

- Now, you have to connect your device to a cellular or Wi-Fi network or iTunes to activate your phone and continue with the setup. You should have inserted the SIM card before turning on the phone if going with the cellular network option. To connect to a Wi-Fi network, just tap the name of your Wi-fi and it connects automatically if there is no password on the Wi-fi. If there is a security lock on the Wi-fi, the screen would prompt you for the password before it connects.

- Next is to manually set up your iPhone XR by tapping **"Set up Manually"**. You can choose the **"Quick Start"** option if you own another iOS 11 or later device by following the onscreen instruction. If you don't have this, then set up your iPhone manually.
- To set up manually, read the Data and Privacy Information from Apple and then click on **"Continue"**.
- Click on *"Enable Location Services"* to grant access to apps like **Maps** and **Find my Friends**. This option can be turned off whenever you want. You would see how to turn on the location services and how to turn it off completely on your iPhone in a later part of this book. You can also click on *"Skip Location Services"*, if you wish not to set this feature yet.

- The next step is to set up Face ID. You would need the Face ID to unlock your device as well as authenticate your purchases.

- To set up the Face ID at this stage, click on Continue and follow the instructions you see on your screen. You can also do this step later by clicking on **"Set Up Later in Settings."** The steps to do this after this stage is included in this guide.

- Next step is to register alternate face. You can either add another appearance of yourself or add a friend or family member as an alternate face. Setting an alternate face can be helpful for times when the device is unable to recognize you because of a change in appearance. To do this, go to Settings, then click on "Appearances" and then click on *"Set Up an Alternative Appearance"* to complete the registration

- Whether you register the Face ID now or not, you would need to create a personal four digits code to protect your device. With this passcode, you would be able to access Face ID and Apple Pay. Tap

"**Passcode Option**" if you would rather set up a four-digit passcode, custom passcode or even no passcode.

- With an existing iTunes or iCloud backup or even an Android device, you can move your backed-up data to the new device or move contents from the old to the new smartphone. If you wish to restore via iCloud, select "**Restore from iCloud Backup**" or select "**Restore from iTunes Backup**" for restoring from iTunes. However, if this is your first smartphone, simply select "**Set Up as New iPhone**".

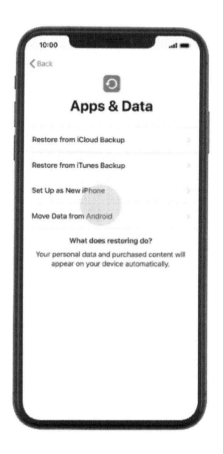

- To proceed, you need to input your Apple ID. For those with an existing Apple account, simply put in your ID and password to sign in. If you have no existing Apple ID or maybe you have forgotten your login details, click on **Don't**

have an Apple ID or forget it. If you have more than one Apple ID, you should choose the option **Use different Apple IDs for iCloud & iTunes**

- On the next screen, accept the iOS terms and conditions to move on.
- Next item is to set up Siri and other services you would need on your device, Siri has to be trained to recognize your

voice so you would have to speak few words to Siri. You can also choose to set up the iCloud keychain and Apple Pay at this point.

- Also, set up screen time to inform you on how much time you spend on your device. You may also set time limit for the length of time you make use of apps.
- Next is to turn on automatic update and other needed features
- Now click on **"Get Started"** to finish this startup and begin to enjoy and explore your new smartphone.

Screen Icons, Buttons and Sockets

Wi-Fi icon: this icon notifies you that you are connected to Wi-fi.

Data Connection Icon: when you see this icon on your device, it means you have an active data connection.

Network Mode Icon: This gives you the strength signal of your network connection. The More the bars, the stronger your connection.

Flight Mode icon: whenever you are on flight mode, this icon shows on the screen.

Signal Strength icon: shows the strength of your connection per time.

Battery Charging icon: with this icon, you know that your phone battery is charging.

Battery Icon: this would only show the level of your battery without showing the percentage. I would show you how to see the percentage level later in the book.

Silent Mode Key: This key is at the top left side of the device; you can slide the key up or down to enable or disable the silent mode. No sound notification would occur on your device whenever the silent mode is activated

Side button: This button was previously referred to as the **"Sleep/ Wake"** button and it can be found at the top right side of the iPhone. With this button, you can power on your device and also turn on screen lock.

Camera lens: for taking beautiful pictures and videos.

Volume keys: With these keys located at the left side of your iPhone, you can control the volume when listening to music, on call or to adjust the ring volume. It also works to mute incoming call alert.

Lightning port: this socket is placed at the bottom of the device for charging your phone or to plug in headset for listening to music or for handsfree call.

How to Insert SIM in iPhone XR

Before you power on your new device, it is important that you first insert the SIM. Follow the steps below to do this:

- In your iPhone pack, you would see a Pin-like opener which you would need to open both the SIM and memory card holder.
- Insert the opener into the tiny hole in the SIM holder.
- Pull out the SIM holder once the opener is able to clip it out as seen in the image above.
- When placing your SIM, ensure that the angled corner of the SIM is placed in the angled corner of the SIM holder. With the iPhone XR, you can only use Nano SIMs.
- Once done, push the SIM holder back to its correct position and your SIM is ready for use.

How to Extend the Device Battery Life

There are some apps and services that makes use of lots of power which would quickly drain the battery life. You can choose to turn on low power mode to reduce the power consumption.

- From **Settings**, go to **Battery**.
- Turn the switch beside **Low Power Mode** to the right to enable it.
- Go to Home screen.

How to Charge the Battery for the iPhone XR

You need to charge your phone when needed for it to be always available for use. Do not wait for the battery to drain before charging as this can spoil the battery. At the top right side of the screen, you would see your battery level. The more the colored section, the more power the device have and vice versa.

- Connect the phone charger to a power socket and then connect the USB side to the lightning port at the bottom of the phone.
- Check that you can see the battery charging icon at the top of the screen to alert you that the phone is charging.

How to turn off iPhone XR

Follow the steps below to turn off your iPhone XR:

- Hold both the volume down and the side button at same time.

48

- As soon as you see the power off slider as shown in the picture below, release the buttons.
- Move the slider to the right for the phone to go off.
- You may also use the side and volume up button, only thing is, you may take a screenshot in error rather than shutting down the phone.

How to turn on iPhone XR

The following steps would show how to turn on the iPhone XR:

- Press the **Side** button until the iPhone comes on.
- Release the button once the Apple logo appears and allow your iPhone to reboot for about 30 seconds.
- Once the iPhone is up, you would have to input your password if you have one.

Going Home on your iPhone XR

- No matter where you are on your smartphone, simply swipe the screen from the bottom up to return to the home screen.

How to Set/ Change Language on iPhone XR

- From the Home screen, click on the **Settings** option.
- Select **General** on the next screen.
- Then click on **Language and Region.**

- Click on **iPhone Language** for options of available languages.
- Select your language from the drop-down list and click on **Done**.
- A pop-up would appear on the device screen to confirm your choice. Click on **Change to (Selected Language)** and you are done!

How to set up Apple ID on iPhone XR

- Navigate to the **Settings** option.
- At the top of your screen, click on **Sign in to your iPhone.**
- Select the option "**Don't have an Apple ID or forgot it?"**
- Once you see a pop-up on the screen, click on **Create Apple ID**.
- Input your date of birth and click on **Next**.
- Input your first name and last name then click on **Next**.

- The next screen would present you with the email address option. If you want to create a new email address, select the option **"Get a free iCloud email address"** or Click on **"Use your current email address"** if you want to use an existing email.
- For the existing email address, input your existing email address and password.
- If creating a new one, click on the option and set your preferred email and password.
- Verify the new password.
- Next step is to select 3 Security Questions from the list and provide answers that you would not easily forget.
- Agree to the device's Terms and conditions to proceed.
- Select either **Merge** or **Don't Merge** to sync the data saved on iCloud from reminders, Safari, calendars and contacts.

- Click on **OK** to confirm the **Find My iPhone is turned on.**

How to use Siri on iPhone XR

Everyone simply loves working with Apples' virtual assistant, everyone loves Siri. For most users, they spend their time asking her questions while she provides answers but she can offer more than answering questions.

1. **How to Set up Siri on iPhone XR**

You have to set up Siri, just like you set up the Face ID. Find below the steps to do this on your iPhone XR:

- Click on **Siri & Search** from the **Settings** app.
- Next to the option **"Press Side Button for Siri",** move the switch to the right to activate the function.
- A pop-up notification would appear on the screen, select **"Enable Siri"**.

- Switch on the **"Listen to Hey Siri"** option and follow the instructions you see on the screen of your iPhone. (activate the **Allow Siri When Locked** option if you would like to use Siri when your iPhone is locked).
- Click on **language** and select the desired language.
- Click on the **"Siri & Search"** button at the top left of the screen to go back.
- Scroll and select **Siri Voice.**
- On the next screen, select **"accent and gender."**
- Click on the **< Siri & Search** button at the top left of the screen to go back.
- Select **"Voice Feedback"**.
- Choose your preferred setting.
- Click on **"< Siri & Search"** at the top left of the screen.
- Select **"My Information."**
- Click on the contact of choice. If you set yourself as the owner of the phone, the

device would use your data for various voice control functions like navigating home. You can create yourself on the contact by following the steps given in creating contact.

- Select the desired application.
- Next to **"Search and Siri Suggestions"** slight left or right to turn on or off.
- And Siri is set up and ready for use!

2. How to Activate Siri on the iPhone XR

You have two ways to activate the Siri feature

- Voice option. If you enabled "Hey Siri", then you can begin by saying "Hey Siri" and then ask Siri any question.
- Using the side button. To wake Siri, press the side button and ask your questions. Release the side button once done for Siri to stop listening

3. How to Exit Siri

To exit Siri, follow the simple step below.

- Press the side button or swipe u from the bottom of the display to exit Siri.

How to Set Up Apple Pay

You have to be on the latest iOS version to be able to use the Apple Pay. Once you are sure that your device is updated, then follow the steps below:

- First thing you should do here is to add your card, either debit, credit or prepaid cards to your iPhone.
- You should be signed into the iCloud using your Apple ID.
- To use the Apple Pay account on multiple devices, add your card to each of the devices.

To add your card to Apple Pay, do the following:

- Go to Wallet and click on ⊕
- Follow the instructions on your device screen to add a new card. The iPhone XR

allows you to add as much as 12 cards. You may be asked to add cards that is linked to your iTunes, cards you have active on other devices or cards that you removed recently. Chose the cards that fall into the requested categories and then input the security code for each card. You may also need to download an app from your card issuer or bank to add your cards to the wallet.

- When you select **Next,** the app would pass the information you inputted through your bank or card issuer to verify and confirm that the card can be used on Apple Pay. Your bank may contact you first before they verify the card.

- After the card is verified, click Next to begin using Apple Pay.

How to check out with Apple Pay

Here are useful steps to check out on Apple Pay for your daily transactions:

- When you are ready to make your payments using the Apple Pay, simply double-press the side button to open the Apple Pay screen.
- Stare into the screen of your smartphone to verify with Face ID (or manually enter your passcode).
- Then place the iPhone XR close to the payment terminal.
- If using Apple Pay Cash, double-press the side button to approve the payment.

How to Set/ Change Date/ Time on iPhone XR

- From the Home screen, click on the **Settings** option.
- Select **General** on the next screen.
- Then click on **Date & Time.**

- On the next screen, beside the "**Set Automatically**" option, move the switch right to turn it on.
- Slide the page from bottom up to return back to Home screen.

How to Use the Control Centre

- From the right side of the notch, swipe down to go to the control center.
- Click on the desired function to either access it or turn it on or off.
- Move your finger up on the needed function to choose the required settings.
- Once done, swipe up to return to home screen.

Settings for Control Centre

- Go to Settings> Control Centre.
- On the next screen, beside the **Access within Apps** option, move the switch to turn it on or off.
- Click on **Customize Controls.**

- For each function you want to remove, click on the minus (-) sign.
- To add icon under **More Controls,** click on the plus (+) sign at the left of each of the icons you want to add.
- Click on the move icon beside each function and drag the function to the desired position in the control centre.
- And you are done.

CHAPTER 2: BASIC FUNCTIONS

How to Sleep and Wake Your iPhone XR

Sleeping and waking your iPhone XR will help the battery life to stay longer as well as protect the battery. I have outlined below the steps you should take to put your device to sleep or to wake your device.

- You have two options to wake your iPhone XR and to see the lock screen; You can either tap the screen or just take up the device and glance into the phone to wake the iPhone XR.

- Once the lock screen is shown, you have the option of accessing the camera or the flashlight without having to unlock your phone. To do this, tap and hold the individual icon until you hear a click sound.

- When you are no longer using the device, simply press the side button to put it to sleep. If you have the iPhone XR customized Apple Leather Folio case, you can just open the case to wake and close the case to sleep your device.

How to Set up Face ID on iPhone XR

The Face ID allows you to perform several functions by just glancing at your device. You can sign into apps, unlock your smartphone, authorize your purchases and several other options. Once you are ready to set up the Face ID, check that nothing is covering either your face or the TrueDepth camera. You can have your contacts and glasses on when setting up this feature. For the best result, put your iPhone about an arm's length from your face.

- To setup the Face ID, go to Settings from the Home screen
- Click on **"Face ID and Passcode"**
- Then enter the passcode
- Then click on "*Set Up Face ID*"
- Select "*Get Started.*"

- Position your face to fit into the circle in the screen, then move your head slowly in a circular motion. Tap **Accessibility Options** if you are not able to move your head.
- Click on "Continue" and repeat the step again
- Once satisfied, click on "Done" to finish up

- If you do not already have a passcode set, you would be prompted to create one as an alternative option for identity verification.

- Go to **Settings** then **Face ID & Passcode** to activate features to go with the Face ID. This includes iTunes & App Store; iPhone Unlock and Safari AutoFill.

How to Unlock your iPhone XR using Face ID

The amazing thing about the iPhone XR is the ability to unlock the device using your Face ID. Follow the steps to unlock your iPhone.

- Go to **Settings** then **Face ID & Passcode.**
- Go to the option **"Use Face ID For"** and switch on **iPhone Unlock.**
- To unlock your iPhone, you need to first wake the device then you glance into the screen.
- The iPhone XR would automatically scan your face and authorize the login attempt.
- Once successful, the **lock icon** on the phone screen will open.
- Swipe from the bottom of the iPhone up to go to the home screen.

How to Turn PIN On or Off

- From **Settings,** click on **Phone.**
- At the bottom of the screen, click on **SIM PIN.**
- Turn the icon beside SIM PIN to the left or right to put off or on.
- Put in your PIN and click on **DONE**. The default PIN for all iPhone XR is 0000.

How to Change Device PIN

- From **Settings,** click on **Phone.**
- At the bottom of the screen, click on **SIM PIN.**
- To change PIN, click on **Change PIN**.
- Type in your current PIN and click DONE.
- On the next screen, type in the new 4-digit PIN and tap DONE.
- The next screen would require you to input the PIN again and click on DONE.

How to Unblock Your PIN

If you enter a wrong PIN 3 consecutive times, it would block the PIN temporarily. Follow the steps to unblock:

- On the home screen, click on **Unlock.**
- Put in the PUK and click on OK.
- Set a new 4-digit PIN and click **OK.**
- Input the PIN again and confirm.

How to make Purchases with Face ID on iPhone XR

If the iTunes and App Store are activated for Face ID under **Face ID & Passcode,** you can use the Face ID to carry out purchases on the App store, iTunes Store and iBooks store. Follow the steps below.

- Go to any of the stores you want to make the purchase from
- Look for the items you wish to purchase and click on it

- To complete payment, press the **Side** button twice and look at your iPhone XR.
- If approved, you would see a message pop up on your screen showing **Done** with a **Checkmark.**

How to Set Screen Brightness

- From **Settings,** go to **Display & Brightness.**

- Under the **Brightness** option, click on the indicator and drag either to the left or to the right until you get your desired brightness.

- Click on the **>Back** sign.

- Click on **General** then **Accessibility.**

- Next, select **"Display Accommodations".**

- Beside the **Auto-Brightness,** slide the button to the left or right to either switch on or switch off this option.

How to Setup Vibration

- From the Home screen, go to **Settings.**

- Click on **Sounds & Haptics.**

- Toggle the switch next to **"Vibrate to Ring"** to enable or disable vibration when the silent mode is disabled.

- Toggle the switch next to **"Vibrate on Silent"** to enable or disable vibration when the silent mode is enabled.

- Return to the home screen.

How to Control Notification Options

- From Settings, go to **Notifications.**

- Click on **Show Preview** and set to **Always** to be able to preview notification on lock screen.

- To set this to only when the device is not locked, click on the option **"When Unlocked".**

- To disable notification preview, select **"Never".**

- Click on the Back arrow at the top left of the screen.

How to Control Notification for Specific Apps

- From the last step above, Click on the specific application.
- On the next screen, beside **Allow Notifications,** move the slide left or right to enable or disable.

How to Control Group Notification

- Scroll down the page and click on **Notification Grouping.**
- Select any of the 3 options as desired.
- Use the Back button to return.

How to Confirm Software Version

- From **Settings,** go to **General** and click on **About.**

- You would see your device version besides **Version** on the next screen.

How to Update Software

- From **Settings,** go to **General** and click on **Software Update.**
- If there is a new update it would show on the next screen.
- Then follow the screen instruction to update the software.

How to Control Flight Mode

- From the top right side of the screen, slide downwards.
- Tap the aero plane sign representing flight mode icon to turn off or on.

How to Choose Night Shift Settings

- From **Settings,** go to **Display & Brightness.**

- Click on **Night Shift.**

- Beside **Scheduled,** click on the indicator and follow the instruction on the screen to select specific period for the Night Shift.

How to Control Automatic Screen Activation

- From **Settings,** go to **Display & Brightness.**
- On the next screen, beside **Raise to Wake,** move the slide left or right to enable or disable.

How to enable Location Services/ GPS on your iPhone XR

- From the Home screen, choose the **Settings** option.
- Scroll towards the bottom of the page and click on **Privacy.**
- Then click on **Location Services.**
- Click on all the apps you would like to have access to your location data.

- Once selected, chose the option **While Using the App.**

How to Turn off location services on iPhone selectively

If there are any apps you would like to block from accessing your location, you can easily turn off location service for such apps by following the steps below.

1. Go to settings on the phone.
2. Move down to the **Privacy** option and then select **Location Services.**
3. You would see all the apps that have access and don't have access to your location. For the apps you wish to access your location information, find such apps, click on them and select **While Using the App.** For the apps you do not wish to access your location information, find such app, click on it and select **Never.** You can also use these steps for the system

73

services you wish not to grant access to your location information.

How to Turn off location services on iPhone completely

If you do not want any apps or systems on your iPhone to access your location information, follow the steps below to disable it:

- Go to **settings** on the phone.
- Move down to the **Privacy** option and then select **Location Services**
- To turn off the location service, all you need to do is toggle the button and then select **Turn off** to confirm the action. This would prevent all apps and system services from gaining access to your location data.

How to Use Music Player

- Click on the **Music Player** icon on the home screen.
- Click on **Playlist** then click on **New Playlist.**
- Tap the text box that has **Description,** type in the name for that playlist.
- Click on **Add Music.**
- Go to the category and click on the audio file you want to add.
- Select **Done** at the top of the screen.
- Select **Done** again.
- Go to the playlist and click on the music.
- Use the Volume key to control the volume.
- Click on the song title.
- Tap the right arrow to go to the next music or the left arrow to go to the previous music.
- Gently slide your finger up the screen.
- Click on shuffle to set it on or off.

- Click on Repeat to set it on or off. Here you can select the number of files you want repeated.

How to Navigate from the Notch

Both the sensors and the Face ID cameras are located in the notch found at the top of the device screen. With the notch, you are able to tell the difference between two important gestures which are the notification center and the control center.

1. **Steps to View Notification Center**

You can access the notification center by swiping down from the notch itself or from the left side of the notch.

2. **Steps to View Control Center**

From the right side of the notch, swipe down to view the control center.

Although the notch has occupied most of the space meant for the status bar, however, once you get into the Control center, you would be able to see all the status bar, this includes the percentage of your battery.

How to keep Track of documents

On your iPhone XR, you can access folders and files stored on your iCloud Drive and any other cloud storage services. You can also access and restore folders and files deleted from your device within the last 30 days. There are 3 subsections in the Browse tab and they are:

1. **Locations**: To view files saved in iCloud, simply click on **iCloud Drive**. To view files recently deleted from your device, click on **Recently Deleted**.

   To add an external cloud storage service, you need to first install the app from the App store (Google Drive, Dropbox etc.), then click **Edit** at the right top corner of your device screen to activate it. Once done, click on **Done**.

Other available options for folders and files are:

- To view the content of a folder, click on the folder.
- To Copy, Rename, Duplicate, Delete, Move, Tag, Share or Get info of a folder or file, simply press the folder or file for some seconds.
- To download items with the cloud and arrow icon, tap on them.
- To annotate a file, simply click on the pencil tip icon at the right upper side of the screen. It is important to know that this feature is only available for select image file formats and PDF.

2. **Favorites:** To add folders to the Favorite section, press the folder for some seconds until a menu pop up, then select **Favorite** from the menu. Currently, you can only do

this from the iCloud Device, and only for folders, no single files.

3. **Tags:** when using macros Finder tags, you will see them in the Tags section. Alternatively, press a file for some seconds to tag such file. Then click **"A Tag Here"** to see all the files that have that tag.

How to Move Between Apps

Switching Apps can be tricky without a home button, but the below steps will make it as seamless as possible.

- To open the App Switcher, swipe up from the bottom of the screen and then wait for a second.
- Release your finger once the app thumbnails appear.
- To flip through the open apps, swipe either left or right and select the app you want.

How to Force Close Apps in the iPhone XR

You do this mostly when an app isn't responding.

- Simply swiping up from the bottom of the screen would show the app switcher. This would display all the open apps in card-like views.

- For iOS 12 users, to force close the app, locate the app from the app switcher and swipe up to close the app.

- For users still on iOS 11, press the app you wish to close for some seconds until you see the red button marked with the minus sign at the top of each app card.

- Tap on the minus button for each of the app you wish to close.

- I would advise you upgrade to iOS 12 to enjoy better features on your iPhone XR.

- To go through apps used in the past, swipe horizontally at the bottom of your home screen.

How to Arrange Home Screen Icons

Follow the steps below to arrange the homes screen icon on your iPhone XR.

- Press and hold any icon until all the icons begin to wiggle.
- Drag the icons into your desired position.
- Tap either the **Done** button at the right upper side of the screen or swipe up to exit the wiggle mode.

How to Choose Network Mode

- From **Settings**, go to **Mobile Data**.
- Select **Mobile Data Options> Enable 4g.**
- To stop using 4g, choose **Off.**
- This option would make your device to automatically switch to either 2g or 3g depending on available coverage.
- Click on **Voice & Data** if you want to use 4g for both mobile data and voice calls.
- Note: To get fast and better connection, use 4g for calls via the mobile network.

- Click on **Data Only** to use for only mobile data.
- Done.

How to set a reminder

Follow the steps below to create a reminder.

1. Open the **Reminder app** on your iPhone XR device.

2. At the top right corner of the screen, click the plus button to create a new reminder or a list.

3. To create a list, tap **List** and tap **Reminder** to create a new reminder.

4. For reminder, enter the exact reminder content.

5. In the content box space, you have two choices.

First option: remind me on a day. With this option, please set the Alarm and Repeat options – Every day, Every week, every month, never etc.,

Second option: Remind me at a location. For this, turn your location on, then set the location you will receive when you arrive or leave.

6. Choose the priority level for the reminder, you can also add notes if needed

7. Chose **Done** to complete the process.

How to set a Recurring Reminder

To create a recurring reminder on your device, follow the steps below:

1. Go to the Reminders app on your device.

2. Type your content on the space for reminder content.

3. Click on the info button beside the new reminder set.

4. Select the option to **"Remind me on a day".**

5. Set the time you want the reminder.

6. Select **Repeat** and then Custom.

7. Set your frequency to Repeat, Weekly, Daily, Monthly or Yearly.

8. Once done, go to **End Repeat** and select date you want the reminder to stop.

How to get Battery Percentage

The iPhone XR does not give room to see the battery percentage of your iPhone always, but you can always get a peek to see your battery percentage. To do this, place your finger at the top-right corner of the iPhone XR display and swipe down to be able to access the Control Center. Once the control center is open, you would see the battery percentage at the top right corner of the page.

Chapter 3: Camera

How to Use Camera

- From the Home screen, tap on Camera
- Move your finger left or right to take you to the **Photo** option which is after Video by your left and before Portrait by your right.
- Click the flash icon at the top left side of the screen to enable flash
- Then move to the next button after Flash to choose your preferred setting
- Set the camera lens at the back of the device to point at the object you want to capture
- Click on the Take Picture icon which is the round icon at the bottom of the screen.
- You can draw two fingers apart or together on the screen to either zoom in or out
- Take the picture

- Return to the Home button once done

How to View Pictures and Video Clips

- Click on **Photos** at the top of the screen
- Once the photo app opens, open the desired folder and then click on the picture or video clip that you want
- Click on the < arrow left to go back to the list of video clips and pictures

How to Use Video Recorder

- Click on the Camera icon
- Move your finger left or right to take you to the **Video** option which is before Photo by your right.
- Tap the Video light icon at the left top of the screen
- Set your desired settings
- Set the camera lens at the back of the device to point at the object you want to capture

- Click on the **Record** icon which is the round icon at the bottom of the screen.
- You can draw two fingers apart or together on the screen to either zoom in or out
- Tap the **Stop** icon at the bottom of the screen to stop the recording
- Return home once done

How to Send Video Clip or Picture in an MMS

You can send a videoclip or picture to another person as an MMS. To do this, follow the listed steps

- Click on Photos
- Go to the desired photo folder
- Click on the desired video clip or picture
- Tap the share button at the left bottom side of the screen with an arrow facing up
- On the next screen, click on **Message**
- On the To field, input the receiver's details

- Click on the Text area to input your message
- Once done, click on the Send button which is the arrow up beside the text box

How to Send Video Clip or Picture in an Email

- Click on Photos
- Go to the desired photo folder
- Click on the desired video clip or picture
- Tap the share button at the left bottom side of the screen with an arrow facing up
- On the next screen, click on **Mail**
- On the To field, input the receiver's details
- Input your email subject on the subject field
- Click on the Text area to input your email message
- Once done, click on **Send** to deliver your email

How to take a Screenshot

Without the home button, taking a snapshot may seem tricky; however, follow these steps to help you take the best shots possible.

- Press both the side and the Volume Up button simultaneously to take a screenshot.

- The photo from the screenshot would be saved automatically in the Photos app, under the **Screenshots** album. Screenshots help you to note down problems you wish to seek help for later.

- To edit the photo, go to the photo and tap the thumbnail at the left bottom corner of your iPhone.

- To view the screenshots in iOS 11, go to **Photos** click on **Albums** then **Camera Roll/ Screenshots**. To do same in iOS 12, go to **Photos,** then **Albums,** go to **Media Types** and select **Screenshots**.

CHAPTER 4: Calls and Contacts

How to Make Calls and Other Call Related Features on Your iPhone XR.

How to Answer Call

- Tap any of the volume keys to silence the call notification when a call comes in.
- If the screen lock is active, slide right to answer the call.
- Click on Accept, if there is no screen lock.
- Tap the end call button at the bottom of the screen once done.

How to Call a Number

- Tap the Phone icon at the left.
- Click on Keypads to show the keypads.
- Input the number you want to call then press the call icon.
- Tap the end call button at the bottom of the screen once done.

How to Call Voicemail

- Click on the phone icon at the left of the home screen.
- Select **Voicemail** at the bottom right corner of the screen.
- Click on **Call Voicemail** in the middle of the screen and listen for the instructions.
- Tap the end call button at the bottom of the screen once done.

How to Control Call Waiting

- From **Settings,** click on **Phone** then **Call Waiting.**
- Move the icon beside it to the left or right to enable or disable call waiting.

How to Control Call Announcement

Your device can be set to read out the caller's name when there is an incoming call. The contact has to be saved in your address book for this to work.

- From **Settings,** go to **Phone** then **Announce Call.**

- Select **Always** if you want this feature when silent mode is off.

- Choose **Headphones & Car** to activate when your device is connected to a car or a headset.

- The **Headphones Only** option would be for when the device is connected to only headset.

- Select **Never** if you do not wish to turn off this feature.

Choosing your Ringtone

- From the Home screen, go to **Settings.**

- Click on **Sounds & Haptics.**

- Then click on **Ringtone.**

- You may click on each of the ringtones to play so you can choose the one you prefer.

- Select the one you like then click the "**<
  Back"** key at the top left of the screen.
- Slide the page from bottom up to return
  back to Home screen.

**How to Add, Edit, and Delete Contacts on iPhone
XR**

The steps below would guide you to add, edit and
delete contacts on your new device.

How to Add Contacts

- At the **Home** screen, select **Extras.**
- Click on **Contacts.**
- Then select the **Add Contact** icon at the
  right upper side of your screen.
- Enter the details of your contact including
  the name, phone number, address, etc.
- Once done inputting the details, tap **Done**
  and your new contact has been saved.

How to Merge Similar Contacts

- At the **Home** screen, select **Extras.**
- Click on **Contacts.**
- Click on the contact you want to merge and click on **Edit.**
- At the bottom of the screen, select **Link Contact....**
- Choose the other contact you want to link.
- Click on **Link** at the top right side of the screen.

How to Save Your Voicemail Number

- Once you insert your SIM into your new device, it automatically saves your voicemail number.

How to Copy Contact from Social Media and Email Accounts

- From Settings, go to **Accounts and Password.**
- Click on the account, e.g. Gmail.

- Switch on the option beside **Contacts.**

How to Add a Caller to your Contact

- On your call log, click on a phone number.
- You would see options to **Message, Call, Create New Contact or Add to Existing Contact**.
- Select **Create New Contact.**
- Enter the caller's name and other information you have.
- At the top right hand of the screen, click on **Done**.

How to Add a contact after dialing the number with the keypad

- Manually type in the numbers on the phone app using the number keys.
- Click on the (+) sign at the left side of the number.
- Click on **Create New Contact.**

- Enter the caller's name and other information you have.

- Or click on **Add to Existing Contact**.

- Find the contact name you want to add the contact to and click on the name.

- At the top right hand of the screen, click on **Done**.

How to Import Contacts

The iPhone XR allows you to import or move your contacts from your phone to the SIM card or SD card for either safekeeping or backup. See the steps below:

- From the Home screen, click on **Settings.**

- Select **Contacts.**

- Chose the option to "**Import SIM contacts**".

- Chose the account you wish to import the contacts into.

- Allow the phone to completely import the contacts to your preferred account or device.

How to Delete contacts

When you remove unwanted contacts from your device, it makes more space available in your internal memory. Follow the steps below.

- From the Home screen, tap on **Phone** to access the phone app.
- Select **Contacts.**
- Click on the contact you want to remove.
- You would see some options, select **Edit.**
- Move down to the bottom of your screen and click on **Delete Contact.**
- You would see a popup next to confirm your action. Click on **Delete Contact** again.
- The deleted contact would disappear from the available Contacts.

How to Manage calls on your iPhone XR

Here, we would talk about how to block calls, set or cancel call forwarding, manage caller ID as well as call logs on your device.

How to Block Calls on the iPhone XR

- Go to **Settings** from the Home screen.
- Click on **Do Not Disturb.** (The DND feature on the iPhone XR allows you determine how you want your device to process incoming calls. The following options are available under DND.
  1. **Do Not Disturb** option – tap on this option to enable or disable the DND feature manually on the device.
  2. Scheduled – To schedule a time for DND to be activate, just tap the tap the time and set the start to end time.
  3. **Allow Calls From** – Use this option only when you want to receive calls from specific people. Select the people and allow calls from them.

4. **Repeated Calls** – This option allows a call to come through once the call is repeated within 3 minutes of the first call.

How to Block Specific Numbers/Contacts on Your iPhone XR

- Click on the **Phone** icon on the Home Screen.
- Tap **Recent** or **Contacts.**
- Select the specific contact(s) or number(s) you desire to block.
- If accessing through **Recent** option, tap the **(i)** icon next to the number.
- Click on **Block This Caller** at the bottom of the screen.
- Click on the **Block Contact** option to confirm your action.
- Blocked contacts or numbers would be unable to reach you.

How to Unblock Calls or Contacts on your iPhone XR

- Go to **Settings** from Home.
- Select **Phone-> Call Blocking & Identification** then click on **Edit.**
- Click on the **minus (-) sign** next to the contact or number you want to unblock.

How to Use and Manage Call Forwarding on your iPhone XR

With the Call Forwarding unconditional (CFU) feature in the iPhone XR, calls can be forwarded to a separate phone number without the main device ringing. This is most useful when you do not wish to turn off ringer or disregard a call but also do not want to be distracted by such calls. To enable this feature, follow the steps below:

- Go to **Settings** from Home.
- Click on **Phone** then **Call Forwarding.**
- Select the **Forward to** option.

- Input the number you want to forward such calls to.
- You can set the calls to be forwarded to voicemail.

Apart from CFU, Call Forwarding Conditional (CFC) allows you to forward incoming calls to a different number if the call goes unanswered on your number. To enable this feature, you need to have the short codes for call forwarding then set the options to your preference. For data on short codes, reach out to your carrier.

How to Cancel Call Forwarding on your iPhone XR

To cancel,

- Go to **Settings** then **Phone**
- Click on **Call Forwarding.**
- Move the slider to switch off the feature.

How to Manage Caller ID Settings and Call Logs on your iPhone XR

You can decide to hide your caller ID when calling certain numbers. Follow the steps below to activate this.

- Go to **Setting** on the Home screen.
- Click on **Phone** then click on **Show My Caller ID.**
- Click on the switch next to **Show My Caller ID** to either enable or disable the option.

When you disable the feature, the called party will not see your caller ID. This is usually for security or privacy reasons.

How to View and Reset Call Logs on your iPhone XR

For every call you make on your device, there is a log saved on the phone app. To view or manage the call log data, follow the steps below:

- On the Home screen, Click on **Phone** to go to the phone app.
- Click on **Recent** then click on **All.**
- Tap on the call log you wish to extract information from.

How to Reset Call Logs

- Go to **Phones,** then click on **Recent>All>Edit.**
- Click on the **minus (-) sign** to delete calls individually.
- To delete the whole call log once, simply tap **Clear** then chose the **Clear All Recent** option.

How to Set Do Not Disturb

Your device can be put to silent mode for defined period. Even though your phone is in silent mode, you can set to receive notification from certain callers.

- Under **Settings,** click on **Do Not Disturb.**

- Toggle the switch next to **"Do Not Disturb"** to enable or disable this function.

- Toggle the switch next to **"Scheduled"** then follow instructions on your screen to set the period for the DND.

- Under **Silence** chose **Always** if you want your device to be silent permanently.

- Select **"While iPhone is locked"** if you want to limit this to only when the phone is locked.

- Scroll down and click on **"Allow Calls from".**

- Chose the best setting that meets your need to set the contacts that can reach you while on DND.

- Click on the back arrow at the top left of the screen.

- Scroll down to **Repeated Calls** and switch the button on or off as needed.

- Click on **"Activate"** under **"Do Not Disturb While Driving"**.
- On the next screen, chose your preferred option.
- Click on the back button to return to the previous screen.
- Scroll down and select **"Auto Reply To"**.
- On the next screen, select the contacts you wish to notify that **Do Not Disturb While Driving** is on.
- Go back to the previous screen.
- Scroll down and select **Auto Reply,** then follow the instructions on the screen to set your auto response message.

CHAPTER 5: Messages and Emails

How to Choose Message Tone on the iPhone XR

- From the Home screen, go to **Settings.**
- Click on **Sounds & Haptics.**
- Then click on **"Text Tone".**
- You may click on each of the message tones to play so you can choose the one you prefer.
- Select the one you like then click the **"< Back"** key at the top left of the screen.
- Slide the page from bottom up to return back to Home screen.

How to Set up your Device for iMessaging

- From Settings, go to Messages.
- Enable iMessages by moving the slide to the right.

How to Compose and Send iMessage

- From the Message icon, click on the new message option at the top right of the screen.
- Under the "To" field, type in first few letters of the receiver's name.
- Select the receiver from the drop down.
- You would see iMessage in the composition box only if the receiver can receive iMessage.
- Click on the "Text Input Field" and type in your message.
- Click on the send button beside the composed message.
- You would be able to send video clips, pictures, audios and other effects in your iMessage.

How to Set up your Device for SMS

- Your device is automatically set up for SMS once you put in your SIM.

How to Compose and Send SMS

- From the Message icon, click on the new message option at the top right of the screen.
- Under the "To" field, type in first few letters of the receiver's name.
- Select the receiver from the drop down.
- Click on the "Text Input Field" and type in your message.
- Click on the send button beside the composed message.

How to Set up Your Device for MMS

- From **Settings**, go to **Messages**.
- Enable **MMS Messaging** by moving the slide to the right.

How to Compose and Send SMS with Pictures

- From the Message icon, click on the new message option at the top right of the screen.

- Under the "To" field, type in the first few letters of the receiver's name.
- Select the receiver from the drop down.
- Click on the "Text Input Field" and type in your message.
- Click the Camera icon at the left side of the composed message.
- From Photos, go to the right folder.
- Select the picture you want to send.
- Click Choose and then send.

How to Hide Alerts in Message app on your iPhone XR

- Go to the **Message app** on your iPhone.
- Open the conversation you wish to hide the alert.
- Click on the (i) button at the upper right corner of the page.
- Among the options, one of it is '**Hide alerts'**, move the switch to the right to

turn on the option (the switch becomes green).

- Select **'Done'** at the right upper corner of your screen. You are good to go!

How to Create Animoji and Memoji

Let your friends know that you have one of the newest iPhones by sending them messages with Memoji or Animoji. Not only is this a way to show off your device strength, it also adds some spices to your conversation.

From the Animoji app inside Messages, you can either create your own image (called the Memoji) or send from the available 20 animated images of emoji-styled characters. Follow these listed steps to do this:

- Go to Messages on your device.
- You can either create a new conversation or click on an existing one.
- Once inside, you would see the Animoji button (the icon with a monkey head) either at the top of your keypad or at the bottom of your screen. Click on the button.
- Move to the right until you get to the button for a **New Memoji.**
- To add a new Memoji, simply tap the + button.

- The following options would display on your screen to set up your new Memoji:

1. Skin: for Freckles and skin color.
2. Head shape: Shape of head as well as age of face.
3. Hairstyle: Style and color for the hair.
4. Eyes: Eye color, shape, and lashes
5. Nose & Lips: lip color, Nose and lip shape.
6. Brows: Select color and style for the eyebrow.
7. Ears: Set the shape for the ear as well as style and color for the earring.
8. Eyewear: color for the lens and frame as well as style for eyewear.
9. Facial Hair: add the mustache, sideburns, and beard style and color.
10. Headwear: Style and color for the headwear.

- Once you have customized your Memoji, click on **Done** to confirm your selections.

How to Send Memoji and Animoji

- Go to the Message folder and click on the conversation you wish to send the Animoji to.

- Click on the Animoji button at the bottom of your screen (the icon with a monkey head)

- Swipe either ways on the character selector till you see your preferred Memoji, which is first on the line or Animoji.

- At the right bottom of your screen, click on the **Record button** (the red round button) to record your message.

- You can stop the recording before the 30 seconds allocated time by clicking on the stop red button.

- Click on the **Bin** button to delete the recorded message or click on the **Arrow Up** button to send your recorded Animoji message.

Note that your recorded Memoji or Animoji can also be shared via social media and other apps.

How to Create New Contacts from Messages On iPhone XR?

- Go to the Messages app.
- Click on the conversation with the sender whose contact you want to add.
- Above the conversation, you would see their phone number.
- Click on the phone number.
- This would show 3 buttons on the screen.
- Click on the **Info** option.
- You would see the number again at the top of the screen, click on it.
- Then click **Create New Contact**.
- Input their name and other details you have on them.
- At the top right hand of the screen, click on **Done**.

How to Set up Your Device for POP3 Email

- From Settings, go to **Accounts and Password**.
- Click on **Add account**.
- Select your service provider from the list or click on others If your service provider is not on the list.
- Select **Add Mail Account.**
- Input your details, name, email address and password.
- Under Description, put in your desired name.
- Click Next at the top right corner of the page.
- The next screen is a confirmation that your email has been set up.
- Follow the on-screen instructions to enter in any extra information.

How to Set up Your Device for IMAP Email

- From Settings, go to **Accounts and Password**.
- Click on **Add account**.
- Select your service provider from the list or click on others If your service provider is not on the list.
- Select **Add Mail Account.**
- Input your details, name, email address and password.
- Under Description, put in your desired name.
- Click Next at the top right corner of the page.
- The next screen is a confirmation that your email has been set up.
- Follow the on-screen instructions to enter in any extra information.
- After this, select **IMAP,**

- Under host name, type in the name of your email provider's incoming server.
- Fill in the username and password for your account.
- Under outgoing host server, type in the name of your email provider's outgoing server.
- Click **Next.**
- Select **Save** at the top right of the screen to save your email address.

How to Set up Your Device for Exchange Email

- From Settings, go to **Accounts and Password**.
- Click on **Add account**.
- Select **Exchange** as your email service provider.
- Input your email address.
- Under Description, put in your desired name.

- Click on **Sign In.**
- Input your email password on the next screen.
- Click on **Sign In.**
- Move the indicator next to the needed data type to enable or disable data synchronization.
- Select **Save** at the top right of the screen to save your email address.

How to Create Default Email Account

- From Settings, go to **Mail** at the bottom of the page.
- Click on **Default Account.**
- On the next screen, click on the email address you wish to set as default.

How to Delete Email Account

- From Settings, go to **Accounts and Password**.
- Click on the email address you want to delete.

- Select **Delete Account** at the bottom of the page.
- On the next screen, click on **Delete from my iPhone.**

How to Compose and Send Email

- From the Home screen, select the Mail icon.
- Click on the back arrow at the top left of the screen.
- Select the email address you want to send the email from.
- Click the new email icon at the bottom right side of the screen.
- On the To field, input the receiver email address and the subject of the email.
- Write your email content in the body of the email.
- To insert a video or picture, press and hold the text input field until a pop-up menu comes up on the screen.

- Click **Insert Pictures or Videos** from the pop-up and then follow the instructions you see on the screen to attach the media.
- To attach a document, select **"Add Attachment"** and follow the instructions you see on the screen.
- Click on **Send** at the right top of the screen.

CHAPTER 6: Manage Applications and Data

How to Install Apps from App Store

- Open the app store and click on search.
- Type in the name of the app in the search field.
- Click on Search.
- Select the desired app.
- Click on **GET** beside the app and follow the steps on the screen to install the app. For paid apps, click on the price to install.

How to Uninstall an App

To uninstall an app,

- click and hold the app until it begins to shake.

- Click on the **Delete** option, then select **Delete.**

With this method, every settings and data about the app would be deleted from your phone.

How to Delete Apps Without Losing the App Data

- From the **Settings,** go to **General.**

- Click **iPhone Storage.**

- Click on the app you wish to uninstall and click on **Offload App.**

- Select **Offload App** again to complete.

How to Transfer Content to your iPhone XR from an Android Phone

You can move contents to your device from an Android mobile phone when you first activate the device or after you did a factory reset. To do this, you would see the **Apps and Data** option on your screen.

- Under **Apps and Data,** click on **"Move Data from Android".**

- You have to install the app **"Move to iOS"** on the android phone before you can move data.

- Click on **Continue** when you have downloaded the app.
- Follow the instructions you see on the screen to move data from the Android to the iPhone XR.

How to Control Offload Unused Apps

You can set your device to uninstall apps that are not used in a long time. The app would be uninstalled without deleting the data from the phone. Follow the steps below:

- From the **Settings,** go to **iTunes and App Store.**

- At the bottom of the screen, beside **"Offload Unused Apps",** move the switch left or right to control it.

How to Control Bluetooth

- From **Settings,** go to **Bluetooth**

- Move the switch beside **Bluetooth** to switch on or switch off Bluetooth.
- To pair with a mobile device, put on the Bluetooth then click on the device you want to pair and follow the steps on the screen to link.

How to Control Automatic App Update

- From the **Settings,** go to **iTunes and App Store.**
- Beside **"Update" option,** move the switch left or right to control it.
- Move to **"Use Mobile Data",** move the switch left or right to enable or disable.

How to Choose Settings for Background Refresh of Apps

- From the **Settings,** go to **General.**
- Click on **Background App Refresh.**

125

- Then click on **Background App Refresh** again.

- Select **OFF** to disable.

- To refresh the apps using Wi-fi, select **Wi-fi.**

- Select **Wi-fi and Mobile Data** if you want to be able to refresh using mobile data.

- Use the back button to return to the previous screen.

- For each of the apps listed, move the slide either left or right to enable or disable.

How to configure your iPhone XR for manual syncing

- Using either Wi-fi or USB, let your device be connected to a computer.
- Manually open the iTunes app if it doesn't come up automatically.
- Tap on the iPhone icon on the top- left of the iTunes screen. If you have multiple iDevice, rather than seeing the iPhone icon, you would see menu showing all the connected iDevices. Once the devices are displayed, select your current device.
- Tap on the **Apply** button at the bottom right corner of your screen.
- Tap on the Sync button if it doesn't start syncing automatically.

What is iCloud Backup?

iCloud is a limited online space that Apple offers to all its users. This means that for every one that have an Apple account, they can enjoy the benefits that comes with using iCloud. With iCloud, you can sync all your Apple devices together. Then, what is iCloud backup. iCloud backup allows you to backup all your apple devices as well as computers on the iCloud. And then you can move data backed on the iCloud to any of your iPhones whenever you need it.

Files that can be backed up on the iCloud include

- Messages (plus SMS, iMessage, MMS)
- App data
- App layout and home Screen
- Visual voicemail
- Call history
- Ringtones
- HomeKit configuration
- Settings
- Videos and photos
- Apple Watch backup
- History of all purchases done on Apple.

Some files are already stored in the iCloud and cannot be backed up again. These files include bookmarks, contacts, notes, mails, iCloud photo library, calendar, shared phots, My Photo Stream and other data stored on the iCloud

How to sign into iCloud on your iPhone XR.

- Go to the **Settings app.**

- At the top of your screen, click on **Sign in to your iPhone**.

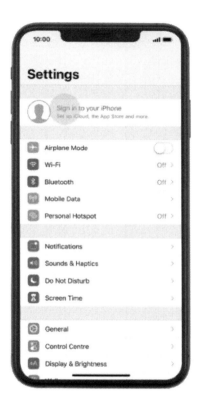

- Enter your Apple ID email address and password.
- Then click on **Sign In.**

- Next screen would ask for your device passcode if you set up one.
- Set the iCloud Photos the way up like them.
- Switch **Apps using iCloud** on or off, however you want it.

How to Sign Out of iCloud on Your iPhone XR

- From the **Settings app,** click on **Apple ID.**
- Click on **Sign Out** at the bottom of the screen.
- Input your Apple ID password then select **Turn Off.**

- Chose the data you would like to keep a copy of on your iPhone and move the switch on.
- At the top right corner of your screen, click on **Sign Out.**
- Click on **Sign Out** to confirm your decision.

How to Use iCloud Backup

To use the iCloud backup, ensure that your device is connected to Wi-fi before you proceed. To back up, follow the steps below

- Navigate to **Settings>Name>iCloud.** If you are using other iOS, go to **Settings>iCloud.**
- Look out for the button titled **'Backup" or "iCloud Backup",** switch it on.
- Ensure your device is connected to Wi-fi and device must be charging during the process.
- Once the backup is done, visit **Settings>Name>iCloud>iCloud Storage>Manage Storage** to confirm the phone backup.

How to share a calendar on iPhone XR via iCloud

To share your calendar on your iPhone, it is important to first of all turn on the iCloud for calendar option. Kindly follow the steps below:

- On your iPhone, go to **'settings'**

- Click on your device name and select "**iCloud**"
- Then turn on "**Calendars**"

After this is done, you can now share your calendar by following these steps

- Open the "**Calendar**" app on your device.
- At the bottom of your screen, select "**calendars**".
- You would see an "**info**" icon next to the calendar you want to share, click on the icon.
1. Select the '**add person**" option on the screen then pick the people you wish to share the calendar with.
2. Tap "add" followed by "Done" at the top of your screen.

How to Synchronize using iCloud

- Click on your Apple ID under Settings.
- Click on iCloud.

- Scroll down to **iCloud Drive** and move the switch left or right to enable or disable.
- Under iCloud, click on **Photos.**
- Scroll down to **Upload to My Photo Stream** and slide left to right to activate or disable.

How to manually add or remove music and videos to your iPhone XR

To manually manage your music and videos, you would have to copy the video files and music tracks to the iPhone from the iTunes Library. Follow the steps below to do this:

- Connect your device to your computer or Mac.
- Launch the iTunes app.
- Manually move the media to the left side of the window.
- Release the media on top of the iPhone (Under Devices).

- Now you can drag any of the items from the main window to the sidebar to add to your iPhone from iTunes.

How to Choose Settings for Find my iPhone

- Click on your Apple ID under Settings.
- Click on iCloud.
- Scroll down and click on **Find My iPhone.**
- Slide left to right to activate or disable.
- Scroll down to **"Send Last Location"** and Slide left to right to activate or disable.

How to Use Find My iPhone

This option helps to recover your iPhone when lost. To activate:

- Open a browser on your computer and go to www.icloud.com
- Select **Find iPhone.**
- At the top middle of the screen, select **All Devices.**

- Select the name of your mobile device from the drop down.
- The next screen would show you your device latest position on the map. (Ensure that you have activated sending of your mobile phone's latest position.)
- Tap **Play Sound**. This would send a signal to your lost device that would play back for 2 minutes. For the play back to happen, your device has to be connected to a strong connection.
- To lock your device, click on **Lost Mode** on the screen and follow the steps to lock the device.
- Not only can you lock your iPhone with a code, you can also set up a lost message to show on the screen of the device.
- To delete all the phone content, select **Erase iPhone.** Once this is done, you would be unable to use Find my iPhone for that device.

How to Downgrade iOS System on Your iPhone

Did you just recently upgrade your iOS but want to go back to the previous iOS you are familiar with? Here, you will learn tips on how to downgrade without loss of data.

1. First, it is important you back up your device data. I would advise you backup using iCloud as backing up with iTunes can affect your device system when you restore. This would make it easy to restore from iCloud once you have downgraded the iPhone.

   To backup, follow the steps below:

- Go to **Settings>iCloud.**
- Look out for the button titled '**Backup" or "iCloud Backup",** switch it on.
- Ensure your device is connected to Wi-fi and device must be charging during the process.
- Once the backup is done, visit **Settings>Name>iCloud>iCloud**

Storage>Manage Storage to confirm the phone backup.

2. Now you are ready to downgrade the system. To downgrade, you need to have a backup file from the iOS you want to switch to. If you don't have any, you can get a standard file downloaded from **Apple Support** to the iOS system. To do this,

- Visit Apple Support, navigate to the Download page
- In the product list, find and select iPhone, then select your desired iOS system.
- Select the option to download to your PC.
- While the file is downloading, update the iPhone on your computer to the most current version.
- Use the lighting cable to connect your phone to your PC.
- On the top left, click the iPhone icon and switch mode to **iPhone Device Panel.**

- Look for the "Restore Backup" button and select it.
- Select the file gotten from the Apple support to downgrade your iPhone to your choice system.
- Once the downgrade is done, you can visit **Setting>General>Software Update** to confirm that the downgrade was done successfully.

3. Once you are done with the downgrade, next is to restore the data saved. Do not worry if you cannot find the data on your iPhone. Just go to the iCloud Backup to restore them. To do this, follow the steps below

- Go to **Settings>General>Reset**.
- Here, you are able to reset the needed data and also **"Erase All Content and Settings"** directly.
- On the App and Data screen, click on "Restore from iCloud"

- Next, input your login details into the iCloud account to choose the backup file you wish to restore.
- Allow it to restore without interruption so that you can get all the files you lost after downgrading.
- That is all there is to downgrading.

CHAPTER 7: Internet and Data

How to Set up your Device for Internet

- Your iPhone picks up internet connection once a SIM card is inserted into the phone.

How to Join a Wi-fi Network

- Go to Settings, then click on Wi-fi.
- Move the switch beside **Wi-fi** to the right to put on the Wi-fi.
- Select your Wi-fi network from the drop down.
- Type in the password and click on **Join.**

How to Control Wi-fi Setup

- From the top right side of the screen, draw down the screen.
- Click on the Wi-fi icon to enable or disable.
- Move the switch beside **Wi-fi** to the right or left to put off or on.

How to Use Internet Browser

- Click on the internet browser icon.

- Go to the address bar at the top of the page and input the web address. Then tap Go.

- Click on the menu icon at the bottom of the screen.

- Click on **Add Bookmark.**

- Under Location, click on Favorites and click on Bookmarks.

- Type in the name for the page you want to save and click on save.

- Tap the bookmark icon next to the menu icon.

- Click on the website under bookmark you want to visit.

How to Check Data Usage

- Go to **Mobile Data** under **Settings**.

- Beside **Current Period**, you would see your data usage on the device.

- Under each app, you would see the data usage for those apps.

How to Clear Browser Data

- Go to Settings, then click on **Safari.**
- On the next screen, click on **Clear History and Website Data.**
- From the pop-up, click on **Clear History and Data.**

How to Control Mobile Data

- Go to **Mobile Data** under **Settings.**
- Move the switch beside **Mobile Data** to the right or left to put off or on.
- Scroll to where you have the applications and move the switch beside each app to the right or left to put off or on.

How to Control Data Roaming

- Go to **Mobile Data** under **Settings.**
- Click on **Mobile Data Options.**
- Move the switch beside **Data Roaming** to the right or left to put off or on.

How to use your iPhone as a Hotspot

- Go to **Personal Hotspot** under **Settings**.

- Move the switch beside **Personal Hotspot** to the right or left to put off or on.

- IF wi-fi is disabled, click **Turn on Wi-fi and Bluetooth.**

- Select **Wi-fi and USB only** if wi-fi is enabled already.

- Input the wi-fi password beside the field for wi-fi password.

- Select **Done** at the top of the screen.

How to Control Automatic Use of Mobile Data

- Go to **Mobile Data** under **Settings**.

- Move the switch beside **Wi-fi Assist** to the right or left to put off or on.

CHAPTER 8: Using Apps on the iPhone XR

How to Install Facebook

To be able to use Facebook on your device, your device has to be connected to the Internet along with an active Apple ID account. Follow the steps below to install Facebook

- Go to the App Store
- Click on the search icon
- Click on the search field
- Type in **Facebook** and begin search
- Once the search result returns, click on Facebook
- Next, click on **GET**
- Follow the instructions you see on your screen to successfully install the app
- Return to the Home screen once done

How to Use Facebook App

- Click on the Installed Facebook app

- If its your first time to access it on this device, you would be required to put in your login details
- Click on the field (What is on your mind)
- Then enter your text
- Click on **Share** at the top right once done
- If you want to share a photo, return to the home screen and select the **Photo icon** to take you to your picture album
- Select the picture or video clip you want to share
- Click on **Done**
- Type in your text in the txt field and click on **Share**
- To Check in on Facebook, return to the home page and click on the **Check In** icon
- Click on the **Search field**
- Type the name of your location and then select the correct location as applies
- Click on the text field if you would want to input text

- Write your message then share
- To chat on Facebook, click on the Facebook Messenger bar at the top right of your screen while in the app
- Click on the New Message icon at the top right of the screen
- Click on the TO field and put in the recipient name, click on the name from the dropdown
- Type your message in the text field
- Then click on the Send button beside the text field

How to Install Gmail

- Go to the App Store
- Click on the search icon
- Click on the search field
- Type in **GMAIL** and begin search
- Once the search result returns, click on Facebook
- Next, click on **GET**

- Follow the instructions you see on your screen to successfully install the app
- Return to the Home screen once done

How to Use GMAIL

- Click on the Installed GMAIL app
- If it is your first time to access it on this device, you would be required to put in your login details
- Click on the new email icon at the bottom right of the screen
- Click on the TO field to input the receiver email address
- On the Subject field, input the subject of your email
- Input the body of your email in the text field
- Then click on the **SEND** icon to send
- To reply an email, click on the email

- Click the reply button at the bottom of the screen
- Input your text in the text field
- Then click on the **SEND** icon

How to Install YouTube

- Go to the App Store
- Click on the search icon
- Click on the search field
- Type in **YouTube** and begin search
- Once the search result returns, click on Facebook
- Next, click on **GET**
- Follow the instructions you see on your screen to successfully install the app
- Return to the Home screen once done

How to Use YouTube

- Click on the Installed YouTube app

- If it is your first time to access it on this device, you would be required to put in your login details
- Click on the upload icon at the top of the screen
- Select the video clip you want to upload
- The next screen would show you steps on how to edit your video, click on **Next** once done
- Click on the text field and input your text
- Click on **Upload** once done
- To search for a video, click on the search icon at the top right of the screen
- Type in the search word in the search field and click on **Search**
- Click on the video clip you want to access
- Play or add to playlist

How to Install Twitter

- Go to the App Store

- Click on the search icon
- Click on the search field
- Type in **Twitter** and begin search
- Once the search result returns, click on Facebook
- Next, click on **GET**
- Follow the instructions you see on your screen to successfully install the app
- Return to the Home screen once done

How to Install Google Map

- Go to the App Store
- Click on the search icon
- Click on the search field
- Type in **Google Map** and begin search
- Once the search result returns, click on Facebook
- Next, click on **GET**
- Follow the instructions you see on your screen to successfully install the app
- Return to the Home screen once done

How to Use Google Map

- Click on the Installed Google Map app
- Click on the search field and input your desired address
- Select your destination from the dropdown list
- At the bottom of your phone screen, select your destination
- You would need to login to your Google account if you wish to save this location as a favorite
- Once the address opens up, click on Save
- A list would come up on your screen, select your preferred settings either favourite, Want to go, Starred places or New List.
- If you selected New List, follow the steps on your screen to create a new list
- Next, click on **Directions**
- At the top of your screen, tap your mode of transport

- Select your preferred route
- Click on **Start** by the bottom right side of the screen
- At the bottom of the screen, you would see travel information showing estimated time of arrival, travel time and distance to location.
- Once done, click on **Exit** at the bottom right of the screen

CHAPTER 9: Troubleshooting the iPhone XR Device

Most challenges encountered with the iPhone XR can easily be resolved by restarting your device. However, in this section, we would look at every possible challenge you may have with the iPhone XR and the solutions.

Complete iPhone XR Reset Guide: How to perform a soft, hard, factory reset or master reset on the iPhone XR

Most minor issues that occur with the iPhone XR can be resolved by restarting the device or doing a soft reset. If the soft reset fails to solve the problem, then you can carry out other resets like the hard reset and master reset. Here, you would learn how to use each of the available reset methods.

How to Restart your/ Soft Reset iPhone

This is by far the commonest solutions to many problems you may encounter on the iPhone XR. It helps to remove minor glitches that affects apps or iOS as well as gives your device a new start. This option doesn't delete any data from your phone so you have your contents intact once the phone comes up. You have two ways to restart your device.

Method 1:

- Hold both side and Volume Down (or Volume Up) at the same time until the slider comes up on the screen.

- Move the slider to the right for the phone to shut down.

- Press the **Side** button until the Apple logo shows on the screen.

- Your iPhone will reboot.

Method 2:

- Go to **Settings** then **General.** Click on **Shut Down.**
- This would automatically shut down the device.
- Wait for some seconds then Hold the **Side** button to start the phone.

How to Hard Reset/ Force Restart an iPhone XR

There are some cases when you would need to force-restart your phone. These are mostly when the screen is frozen and can't be turned off, or the screen is unresponsive. Just like the soft reset, this will not wipe the data on your device. It is important to confirm that the battery isn't the cause of the issue before you begin to fore-restart.

Follow the steps below to force-restart:

- Press the **Volume Up** and quickly release.
- Press the **Volume Down** and quickly release.

- Hold down the Side button until the screen goes blank and then release the button and allow the phone to come on.

How to Factory Reset your iPhone XR (Master Reset)

A factory reset would erase every data stored on your iPhone XR and return the device back to its original form from the stores. Every single data from settings to personal data saved on the phone will be deleted. It is important you create a backup before you go through this process. You can either backup to iCloud or to iTunes. Once you have successfully backed up your data, please follow the steps below to wipe your phone.

- From the **Home** screen, click on **Settings.**
- Click on **General.**
- Select **Reset.**
- Chose the option to **Erase All Content and Settings**.

- When asked, enter your passcode to proceed.
- Click **Erase iPhone** to approve the action.

Depending on the volume of data on your phone, it may take some time for the factory reset to be completed.

Once the reset is done, you may choose to setup with the **iOS Setup Assistant/Wizard** where you can choose to restore data from a previous iOS or proceed to set the device as a fresh one.

How to Use iTunes to Restore the iPhone XR to factory defaults

Another alternative to reset your phone is by using iTunes. To do this, you need a Computer either Mac or Windows that has the most current version of the iOS as well as have installed the iTunes software. Factory reset is advisable as a better solution to major issues that come up from software that wasn't solved by the soft or force restart. Although you would lose data, however, you get more problems fixed including software glitches and bugs.

Follow the guide below once all is set:

- Use the Lightning Cable or USB to connect your device to the computer.

- Open the iTunes app on the computer and allow it to recognize your device.

- Look for and click on your device from the available devices shown in iTunes.

- If needed, chose to back up your phone data to iTunes or iCloud on the computer.

- Once done, tap the **Restore** button to reset your iPhone XR.

- A prompt would pop-up on the screen, click **Restore** to approve your action.

- Allow iTunes to download and install the new software for your device.

Troubleshooting Basic Functions

How to Troubleshoot if iCloud isn't Working

If your iCloud isn't working, follow the steps below:

- Ensure the Wi-fi is connected and strong as this is usually the main reason if iCloud backup does not respond.

- Once done, confirm that you have sufficient space in the cloud. Apple gives you only 5G free. If you have used up the free space, clear the files you don't need or rather back them up with iTunes then remove them from the iCloud backup.

- If you do not wish to delete any information, next step would be to purchase additional room in the iCloud. The pricing is shown below:

50 GB per month: 0.99 USD

200GB per month: 2.99 USD

2 TB per month: 9.99 USD

- Finally, remove any irrelevant data from the iPhone or computer before you perform the iCloud backup.

I Can't Activate my Mobile Phone

There are four possible reasons for this. Reasons and solutions are listed below:

- If the activation was not done properly, repeat the activation steps as instructed in this book

- There may be a temporal problem with your network connection. Wait for some time and try again or you can move to any location and then try again.

- The problem may be with the SIM card. If so, contact your carrier's customer service for assistance.

How to Fix "My iPhone is not coming on"

There are 3 possible reasons for this and their solutions:

- The battery may be damaged. If so, get a new battery.

- The battery may have gone down, plug to a power socket and charge the battery.

- Your mobile phone didn't start up correctly: Press and hold the Side button until the phone comes up. Swipe up the screen from the bottom. Input your Sim PIN if it is locked. The default password is 0000. If you type in an incorrect PIN three times, your SIM would be locked and you would need your PUK key to unlock. You can get this from your carrier's customer care. It's important to know that if you put in the wrong PUK number 10 times, it would automatically block the SIM.

My Mobile Phone Doesn't Respond

1. **There may be an issue with the iOS:** restart the device.

Screen lock is on: disable screen lock. Follow the steps below to disable screen lock.

- Press the **Side button.**

- Slide your fingers up the screen.

To set automatic screen lock:

- From **Settings,** go to **Display & Brightness.**

- Click on **Auto-Lock** and chose your preferred settings.

My Device Memory is Full

Applications usually take up more space in our device than other services. You can remove all the apps you do not need or delete all irrelevant items in the phone taking up space. To uninstall an app, click and hold the app until it begins to shake. Click on the **Delete** option, then select **Delete.**

How to Delete Apps Without Losing the App Data

- From the **Settings,** go to **General.**

- Click **iPhone Storage.**

- Click on the app you wish to uninstall and click on **Offload App.**

- Select **Offload App** again to complete.

My Device's Battery Life is Short

There are 14 possible reasons for this as listed below:

- Turn off live wallpapers

- Disable auto app update. Go to **Settings>iTunes & App Store.** Move the slider beside the **"Updates"** option to the left or right to switch on or off. Move the slider beside the **"Use Mobile Data"** option to the left or right to switch on or off. Return to home screen.

- The auto screen lock may be disabled. If so, follow the steps discussed in this book to enable it.

- Your battery may be damaged and you would need to replace it

- The device is programmed to auto sync content. Disable this feature

- Turn off mobile data when not in use

- If the Bluetooth is active, it would drain the battery quickly, switch off the Bluetooth when not in use. Use the steps in this guide.

- Check that the screen brightness is not too high, if it is, lower the brightness.

- Turn off notifications

- Turn off Wi-fi when not in use or when you need to reserve the battery

- You have multiple applications running at the background. Close the ones you are not using

- If GPS is on, you may disable it to save the battery

- Disable vibration if on.

My Mobile Phone is Slow

Possible reasons and their solutions are:

- You may have numerous apps running in the background at same time. Close the ones not in use with our guide on how to do this.

- Your device may be overloaded and you would need to restart the device.

What to do When You can't make Voice Call

The possible reasons and solutions to this are listed below:

- The problem may be from the side of the receiver. Try calling another number to confirm this.

- Check your device to see if the icon for network coverage is on. If there is no network coverage, you can postpone the call till when there is better network.

- You may have network coverage but if the coverage is poor, you would be unable to make calls. You can postpone the call till when there is better network.

- Check that you have sufficient airtime on your prepaid line. Top up credit if you do not have sufficient airtime.

- Check your phone screen to see if flight mode is activated. If active, disable it.

- Your SIM may be bad, you should contact customer service for replacement.

- Your number may have been suspended. Reach out to customer service to activate reactivate your line.

- The selected network on your phone is not in range. Activate the automatic network selection option.

- Your device is overloaded. Restart your device.

No Ringtone is Heard on Incoming Calls

First step is to confirm that you can make calls then check that your phone volume is not muted and that the phone volume is high. Once these steps are done, you should hear the ringtones for incoming calls.

Connectivity Troubleshooting

I Can't Use Wi-Fi

- There is no established Wi-fi connection. Connect to a working wi-fi network.

- The connection is rejected by the Wi-fi you choose. Talk to the wi-fi admin for the correct connection settings.

- There are no Wi-fi networks available. connect to a working wi-fi network.

- Although your device is connected to a wi-fi, yet you are not logged on. Some wi-fi connections require you to log on before you can connect successfully. Simply go to the browser and attempt to open any webpage. The page would direct you to start page of the wi-fi network. Login using the on-screen instructions.

- Wi-fi is not on. Enable your Wi-fi

I Can't Use my Device Internet Connection

- Data Roaming may be disabled, if so, enable the option.

- If the mobile data is off, switch it on to get connected to the internet
- The problem may be caused by your iOS, simply restart your phone.

My Phone Consumes Mobile Data

Possible problems and solutions are:

- If you activated your **GPS position usage for apps,** disable the position for applications you do not need the service for.

- If your **Auto mobile data usage** is enabled, follow the given steps to disable.

- Disable **Mobile data usage for app** if it is active.

- If you have the **Notifications** option enabled, you can either turn it off totally or disable it for select apps.

- If the **Auto update of apps using mobile data** feature is enabled, follow the steps in this book to disable the option

- Check to see if **Background refresh of app** is enabled, **if yes,** disable the option.

How to fix Bluetooth Not Working on iPhone XR

- Confirm that the Bluetooth accessory is among the list of supported devices on your iPhone. If the Bluetooth device isn't supported, you would be unable to connect it to your iPhone.

- Ensure that both your iPhone and the Bluetooth device have sufficient power supply. If either of the two devices have low battery, you would be unable to connect the iPhone to the Bluetooth.

- Check to confirm that the Bluetooth on your iPhone and the Bluetooth accessory is on. To check that this on your iPhone, go to **Settings** then select **Bluetooth.** If the Bluetooth is not coming on, simply restart your iPhone.

- Place both the iPhone and the Bluetooth accessory beside each other. The connection would likely not succeed if the distance between the two devices goes beyond the supported distance.
- Put on both the Bluetooth accessory and the iPhone Bluetooth.
- If the connection is still unstable, just disconnect the pairing, that is, unpair both devices and re-pair them again.
- Restart both the Bluetooth accessory and your iPhone.
- If all the steps above fail, you would need to reach out to Apple support.

How to Fix iPhone Red Screen

Some iPhone XR users have complained of getting a red screen when starting their device and then the phone just keeps restarting. I know that this can be very frustrating but do not worry as I will show you some solutions to this.

1. **Fix the Red Screen by Restarting your iPhone**

The simplest solution to this problem is to restart the iPhone with the steps below:

- Hold the Power button until you see "Slide to power off" on your screen.
- Swipe left to right to turn off your iPhone.
- Press and hold the Power button again to turn on iPhone
- After restarting, you can check if the screen will turn to red again.

2. **Fix iPhone Red Screen by Resetting the iPhone**

We have talked about the steps to hard reset or force restart your iPhone. Simply follow that steps here.

- **Fix iPhone Red Screen by Putting the iPhone XR in DFU Mode**

If all the above methods didn't help resolve the red screen issue, then try putting your device into the DFU mode using iTunes. Before you do this, ensure to back up your data as this process would wipe out data from the iPhone XR.

- On your computer, run the iTunes App.

- Connect your device to the computer.

- Put off the iPhone XR.

- In quick intercessions, press the **Side** button for about 3 seconds and then hold down the Volume Down button for 10 seconds, after which you release the Side button while still holding down the Volume Down button until the screen goes completely black.

- Once the screen is black means the device has gone into DFU mode.

Calls and Voicemail Troubleshooting

How to Fix "I Can't Listen to my Voicemail"

- This may be because you have not set up your voicemail. Set up your voice mail.

- If you are attempting to listen to your voicemail from another mobile, ask your carrier to guide you on how to do this successfully.

How to Fix "I am not Receiving Messages on my Voicemail"

- Your voicemail may not have been activated. If so, call your carrier on how to activate the voicemail.

- You haven't set up calls to the voicemail. Set up calls to be diverted to voicemail whenever you are not available to answer your calls.

How to Fix "I Can't Receive Voice Calls"

- You may have activated the **Divert All Calls** option**,** go back to settings to disable the option.

- It may be a connection problem, if so, simply restart the device.

- It could be that the device diverts missed calls too quickly, simply set up **Divert Delay.**

Messages and Email Troubleshooting

Inability to Send or Receive MMS

- **Data Roaming is disabled:** Turn it on.

- **Problem is from the receiver:** Try sending to a different number.

- **Your mobile phone is not rightly set up for MMS:** follow the right steps stated in this book.

- **Mobile data is turned off:** turn it on.

I am Unable to Send or Receive Messages

Before you take any other step, first check to see if you can make calls. If you are unable to make calls, please follow the tips given on resolving the call problems. If you are able to make calls, it could be any of the reasons listed below along with possible solutions.

- Try to send to another recipient as the challenge may be from the recipient.

- If iMessage is enabled, you may be unable to send SMS. Simply turn off iMessage.

I am Unable to Send or Receive iMessages

- Try to send to another recipient as the challenge may be from the recipient.

- If the Time zone, Date and Time are not Correct, the iMessage would not work. Follow the steps given to set up date and time.

- If the iMessage was not properly activated, it may not function well. Turn off iMessage and activate afresh.

- Your phone may not have been properly set up for iMessages. Follow the steps in this book to set up iMessage.

Entertainment and Multimedia Troubleshooting
How to fix "iPhone won't download and update App" with 5 tips

Confirm the network connection on your iPhone:
If your network connection is unstable or bad, its very likely that the download of apps would pause due to the bad connection. If this is the case, all you need do is change to a faster network or leave the app to download at a better time.

Free up space on your iPhone
If your network is good, then you need to check that you have available space to contain the downloads and updates. If there are no space,

the app would be unable to download or install successfully. To get your device storage, do the following

- Under the "settings" app, select "General"
- Then select "Storage and iCloud Usage".
- Here you can see space used. If all the space has been used up, you can make some space by deleting useless and unwanted files. Once this is done, attempt to download or install afresh.

RE-install app

Another step you can take to fix the download or update issue is to delete the app and download the latest version afresh. Then install it. Before you delete, ensure you back up any needed data.

Check your Apple ID

Confirm that you are successfully signed into the Apple store with the correct details that you use for purchase, for users that have multiple Apple

ID. Alternatively, logout and login afresh to the store.

Try to update the Apps with iTunes

If you have tried to update on iPhone without success, maybe you should try updating via iTunes instead. Follow the steps below:

- Connect your device to your computer and start the iTunes
- At the left-hand side of the iTunes page, you have a drop-down button, select the "Apps" option. Then select Updates at the middle top of the page.
- You have two options to update the apps. Either you select "Update all apps" at the bottom right of the page to update all the apps, or you right click on individual apps and select "update App" to update each app.

Note that if the error is caused by Apple store server, the only thing you can do is to wait for Apple to fix their issues.

I Can't Install Apps

Be sure that you have a working internet network. If no, change your network connection. If yes, follow any of the solutions below:

- The app you wish to download may not be available for download in your country. You may search for a similar app.

- Check your device space to be sure it can contain the app. If there are no sufficient space, delete apps you hardly use, then attempt to install again.

- You may have inputted a wrong Apple ID for your payment. Log into the app store from your computer and input an updated payment information.

- You may not have activated the Apple ID on your device. If so, follow the steps listed in this book to activate Apple ID

I Can't Play Music on my Device

Possible reasons and solutions are below:

- The audio file you are trying to play may not be in a format supported by the phone's music player. Get the file that is accepted by your phone.

- Do a manual check to see if your headset is damaged. Get a new one if damaged.

- You may not have any audio file on your phone. You can move audio from your computer to the phone.

- The audio file may be damaged or broken. Delete the file and send it again from your computer.

I Can't Use GPS Navigation

First step is to check that you have an active working internet connection.

- Your device may be experiencing poor GPS signal. There are a couple of things you can do to fix this: You can either reset your network settings, turn the airplane mode on and off, disable and enable location services, or reset the location and privacy settings.

- Check that GPS is enabled. If its not enabled, go to settings and put it on.

How to Fix Photos Not Showing Up

If you are unable to see your new photos on the iPhone Camera roll, follow the two tips below for help.

Tip 1: Restart iPhone

1. Restart your device.

2. Once the phone is up, take a photo with your phone.

3. In the camera app, click the thumbnail of the photo you took to view the picture.

4. To send this photo via iMessage, tap the **Share** button.

5. Restart the iPhone and then go to the **Photos** app on your iPhone to check for the picture.

Tip 2: Update to the latest version of iOS

It is possible that you are not seeing the photos in the Camera Roll due to a bug in the iOS of your device. To solve this, upgrade to the latest version if you are not already using the most recent version. To do this, visit **Settings > General > Software Update**. You can also explore this tip if your FaceTime live photos are not saving.

Part 2: Solutions to Photos Not Showing Up on iPhone after restore

Tip 1: Perform a restart on iPhone

This is by far the commonest solutions to many problems you may encounter on the iPhone XR. You have two ways to restart your device.

Method 1: Press and hold both the **Side** button and **Volume Up** (or **Volume Down**) at same time until you see a slider on the screen, move the slider for the phone to go off completely and then turn on your device by pressing same buttons.

Method 2: Go to Settings > General > Shut Down, then you see a slider on your screen, move the slider for the phone to go off completely. Hold the **Side** button to power on your iPhone.

Tip 2: Turn on iCloud Photo Library

Did you just restore from iCloud backup and can't find your photos? Its important you know that turning on the iCloud photo library when backing up your iPhone to iCloud means the photos won't be among the items in the iCloud backup. To keep the photos on your restored iPhone, go to **Settings > [name on device] > iCloud > Photos,** then switch on **iCloud Photo Library** before you connect your device to a good Wi-fi connection and allow the iCloud photos to download into your iPhone.

If you did not turn on iCloud Photo Library, all your photos should be included in the backup. To restore back, ensure you have a good Wi-fi connection, then wait patiently for the photos to download into your iPhone.

Part 3: Fixes to iCloud Photos Not Showing Up on New iPhone

Did you move the photos on your old iPhone to iCloud but not able to move the photos to your new device? If you are unable to see the iCloud photos on your new device, simply follow the steps below:

- Check iCloud settings

Turn on the iCloud Photo Library before you begin to download the photos to your iPhone. To check the settings, follow the steps below:

1. Open the **Settings** app on your iPhone.

2. Tap [name on the device]
   > iCloud > Photos.

3. Turn on **iCloud Photo Library**.

4. Ensure your iPhone is connected to a good
   and stable Wi-Fi connection before you
   begin to download the photos.

- **Check the Apple ID on iPhone**

You have to use the Apple ID linked with the old device to sign into the new iPhone. If using the correct one, just sign out of iCloud and sign in again.

- **Check your network connection**

You need a stable Wi-fi connection to be able to sync photos from iCloud to your iPhone. You can change the network connection if your iPhone is connected to a weak connection.

CHAPTER 10: Conclusion

With all the teachings in this book, I am confident that you would be able to fully enjoy all the amazing features of the iPhone XR.

The iPhone XR is not only a phone for making and receiving calls. With the right knowledge on how to use the iPhone XR, you can turn it to your personal office and achieve greater things with this device.

I have ensured that everything you need to know regarding the iPhone XR has been covered in this book from taking the phone out of the box to utilizing every features of the iPhone XR.

If you are pleased with the content of this book, don't forget to recommend this book to a friend.

Thank you.

Printed in Great Britain
by Amazon